T0290509

JOSLYN FLEMING, CHANDRA GARBER, KAREN M. SUDKAMP, ELISA YOSHIARA,
ABIGAIL S. POST, VICTORIA M. SMITH, KHADESIA HOWELL

Women, Peace, and Security in Action

INCLUDING GENDER PERSPECTIVES IN DEPARTMENT OF DEFENSE OPERATIONS, ACTIVITIES, AND INVESTMENTS

For more information on this publication, visit **www.rand.org/t/RRA1696-1**.

About RAND

The RAND Corporation is a research organization that develops solutions to public policy challenges to help make communities throughout the world safer and more secure, healthier and more prosperous. RAND is nonprofit, nonpartisan, and committed to the public interest. To learn more about RAND, visit www.rand.org.

Research Integrity

Our mission to help improve policy and decisionmaking through research and analysis is enabled through our core values of quality and objectivity and our unwavering commitment to the highest level of integrity and ethical behavior. To help ensure our research and analysis are rigorous, objective, and nonpartisan, we subject our research publications to a robust and exacting quality-assurance process; avoid both the appearance and reality of financial and other conflicts of interest through staff training, project screening, and a policy of mandatory disclosure; and pursue transparency in our research engagements through our commitment to the open publication of our research findings and recommendations, disclosure of the source of funding of published research, and policies to ensure intellectual independence. For more information, visit www.rand.org/about/research-integrity.

RAND's publications do not necessarily reflect the opinions of its research clients and sponsors.

Published by the RAND Corporation, Santa Monica, Calif.
© 2023 RAND Corporation
RAND® is a registered trademark.

Library of Congress Cataloging-in-Publication Data is available for this publication.

ISBN: 978-1-9774-1143-3

What Is Women, Peace, and Security?

W omen, Peace, and Security (WPS) is the recognition of
women's impact on peace and security decisionmaking, and the disproportionate impact that conflict has on
women. The goal of WPS is to promote policy initiatives that ensure women's
participation in peace and security, women's adequate protection during
conflict, and the incorporation of gender perspectives into decisionmaking.
The WPS agenda commonly recognizes four pillars: participation, protection,
prevention, and relief and recovery (United States Institute of Peace, undated).
The WPS agenda derived from United Nations Security Council Resolution
(UNSCR) 1325 (UNSCR 1325, 2000). The United Nations resolution recognizes
the critical role that women fill in building sustainable peace and security in
the international arena (United States Institute of Peace, undated). Over the
past two decades, the international community, including the United States,
has worked to further codify the WPS agenda through country National Action
Plans (NAPs) and other legislation.

Within the U.S. Department of Defense (DoD), senior leaders and key
stakeholders identified a need for practical examples that demonstrate how
the principles of WPS are being included in military operations. This report
presents a series of vignettes to help DoD stakeholders understand WPS's
relevance to national security and how WPS principles and gender perspectives have been applied in DoD mission areas. We follow these vignettes with
additional insights based on practitioner input and subject-matter expertise.

*SgtMaj Jennifer L.
Simmons, the sergeant
major of Wounded Warrior
Battalion West, speaks
at a women's leadership
symposium on March 30,
2015, at Marine Corps
Base Camp Pendleton,
California. The symposium
gave junior Marines
a chance to speak to
prominent military leaders
to discuss gender equality
and other topics.*

1

WPS in the United States

The United States adopted two NAPs in 2011 and 2016 that outlined the overarching approach to implementing the UNSCR 1325 principles (Women's International League for Peace and Freedom, undated). Soon after, the United States codified a national strategy for WPS in the Women, Peace, and Security Act of 2017 (or the WPS Act) (Public Law 115-68, 2017). It notes that although women contribute to enhanced conflict prevention and resolution, they are underrepresented in peacebuilding and security processes. As described in the WPS Act, women have had great success in moderating extremism, countering terrorism, stabilizing societies, and resolving disputes through peaceful processes. This incongruous circumstance—that women are crucial to peacebuilding but often missing from the peacebuilding process—underscores the imperative of explicit U.S. policy to promote the inclusion of women in "all aspects of overseas conflict prevention, management, and resolution, and post-conflict relief and recovery efforts" (Public Law 115-68, 2017). Thus, the WPS Act seeks to incorporate women into peace and security decisions not just for the sake of equality but for the overall improvement and sustainment of conflict outcomes. The 2017 legislation also promotes the United States as a leader in supporting the participation of women in conflict prevention and resolution processes beyond its own efforts by partnering with other nations to advance these goals.

FIGURE 1

U.S. Strategy on Women, Peace, and Security Objectives and Lines of Effort

OBJECTIVE 1
Women are more prepared and increasingly able to participate in efforts that promote stable and lasting peace.

OBJECTIVE 2
Women and girls are safer, better protected, and have equal access to government and private assistance programs, including from the United States, international partners, and host nations

OBJECTIVE 3
United States and partner governments have improved institutionalization and capacity to ensure WPS efforts are sustainable and long-lasting.

LINE OF EFFORT 1
Seek and support the preparation and meaningful participation of women around the world in decisionmaking processes related to conflict and crises;

LINE OF EFFORT 2
Promote the protection of women and girls' human rights; access to humanitarian assistance; and safety from violence, abuse, and exploitation around the world;

LINE OF EFFORT 3
Adjust United States international programs to improve outcomes in equality for, and the empowerment of, women; and

LINE OF EFFORT 4
Encourage partner governments to adopt policies, plans, and capacity to improve the meaningful participation of women in processes connected to peace and security and decisionmaking institutions.

SOURCE: Features information drawn from White House, 2019, pp. 5–6.

In line with the requirements of the WPS Act, the U.S. government in June 2019 released its *United States Strategy on Women, Peace, and Security* (White House, 2019),[1] which contains three objectives and delineates four lines of effort that closely align with those discussed in UNSCR 1325 (see Figure 1).

Col. Carolyn Birchfield receives the 402nd Field Artillery Brigade colors from Maj. Gen. Perry Wiggins, former commander of First Army Division West, on July 24, 2012, symbolizing her instatement as the commander of her training brigade.

3

DoD WPS Strategic Framework and Implementation Plan

As one of the agencies tasked with implementing the U.S. Strategy on Women, Peace, and Security, DoD published its *Women, Peace, and Security Strategic Framework and Implementation Plan* (SFIP) (DoD, 2020; U.S. Department of State, undated-b). DoD's plan includes three major objectives that support the WPS strategy's lines of effort (see Figure 2 and Figure 3).

Defense objective 1: DoD exemplifies a diverse organization that allows for women's meaningful participation across the development, management, and employment of the joint force.

Defense objective 2: Women in partner nations meaningfully participate and serve at all ranks and in all occupations in defense and security sectors.

Defense objective 3: Partner nations' defense and security sectors ensure women and girls are safe and secure and that their human rights are protected, especially during conflict and crisis.

FIGURE 2

How DoD Links Global WPS Strategy Lines of Effort to National Strategy and Departmental Equities

GLOBAL	NATIONAL	DEPARTMENTAL
WPS PRINCIPLES • Participation of women in peace and security • Protection of women and girls from violence • Inclusion of women in conflict prevention • Equal access to relief and recover before, during, and after conflict and crisis • Protection of human rights • Equal application of the rule of law • Incorporation of a gender perspective into peace and security efforts	**WPS STRATEGY LOE 1 DIRECTS THE DEPARTMENT TO:** • Seek and support women's meaningful participation in military decisionmaking • Increase the meaningful participation of women in partner nation security sector initiatives, including programs on the rule of law and within professional military education. • Lead by example through inclusion of American women in U.S. efforts abroad. • Leverage relevant analysis and indicators, including the collection of sex-and-age-disaggregated data, to identify and address barriers to women's meaningful participation. **WPS STRATEGY LOE 2 DIRECTS THE DEPARTMENT TO:** • Promote the protection of women and girls' security, human rights, and access to aid with governments and regional or other security sector forces, as appropriate. • Address security-related barriers to the protection of women and girls. • Prioritize efforts to prevent and respond to sexual exploitation and abuse. • Provide women and girls with safe and equal access to humanitarian assistance. • Empower women as partners in preventing and combatting terrorism. **WPS STRATEGY LOE 3 DIRECTS THE DEPARTMENT TO:** • Adjust its international programs to improve outcomes in women's equality and empowerment. • Train DoD personnel on the needs, perspectives, and security requirements of men and women; protecting civilians from violence, exploitation, and trafficking in persons; and international humanitarian law (IHL) and international human rights law (IHRL). • Apply gender analyses to improve DoD program design and targeting. **WPS STRATEGY LOE 4 DIRECTS THE DEPARTMENT TO:** • Encourage partner nation governments to adopt policies, plans, and capacity to improve the meaningful participation of women in processes connected to security and decisionmaking institutions. • Work with partner nations to remove legal, regulatory, and structural barriers faced by women in defense and security sectors. • Assist partner nations in increasing opportunities for women to service in security sector forces, including peacekeeping and military organizations, by developing their technical and professional competencies.	**DoD EQUITIES SUPPORTING WPS PRINCIPLES** • Diversity & Inclusion • Gender Integration • Inclusive Leadership Development • Professionalization of Partner Nation Armed Forces • Recruitment & Retention • Sexual Harassment & Assault Prevention • Sexual Exploitation & Abuse Prevention • Gender-Based Violence Prevention • Protection of Civilians • Protection of Children Affected by Armed Conflict • Countering Trafficking in Persons • Humanitarian Assistance & Disaster Relief • Countering Violent Extremist Organizations • International Humanitarian Law • International Human Rights Law • Protection of Cultural Property

SOURCE: Adapted from DoD, 2020, p. 9.

NOTE: LOE = line of effort.

FIGURE 3

How DoD WPS Objectives Map onto WPS Strategy Lines of Effort

	WPS LOE 1 Support women's participation	WPS LOE 2 Promote women and girls' human rights, safety, and access	WPS LOE 3 Adjust U.S. programming	WPS LOE 4 Encourage partner nations to support WPS
DEFENSE OBJECTIVE 1 Model and Employ WPS	●	●	●	
DEFENSE OBJECTIVE 2 Promote partner nation women's participation	●		●	●
DEFENSE OBJECTIVE 3 Promote protection of partner nation civilians		●		●

SOURCE: Adapted from DoD, 2020.
NOTE: LOE = line of effort.

Our Approach: Vignettes Showing WPS Principles in Action at DoD

DoD seeks to communicate WPS concepts, principles, and framework to personnel across DoD, and to this end, asked us to develop vignettes that can communicate WPS in action in a variety of regions and functions and across the lines of effort. Using the WPS principles outlined in DoD's SFIP (the left column of Figure 2), we gathered the following vignettes[2]—collected from service members and DoD civilians and reflecting their personal perspectives—that demonstrate those principles in action.[3] The vignettes reflect personal experiences of WPS in action across the combatant commands (CCMDs), in a variety of DoD functions, and across multiple WPS lines of effort. Although we offer initial thoughts on the broader impact on WPS, we note that further research and analysis are needed to truly assess how the framework is operationalized within DoD. These stories are meant to provide operational examples and are by no means exhaustive. Finally, these vignettes should not be interpreted as prescriptive because they are often context-specific, although they also illustrate the complex state of WPS implementation throughout DoD.

At the sponsor's request, we focused on vignette identification and collection to highlight WPS principles in operation rather than a broad assessment of DoD's implementation of WPS. In the following sections, readers will encounter vignettes from each of the geographic CCMDs and in a variety of operational contexts. To achieve this goal, vignette outreach was conducted via multiple methods. Initially, we reached out to relevant service and veteran

U.S. Navy PO1 Megan Garcia provides security during a key leader engagement with the director of women's affairs on January 29, 2013, in the city of Farah in Afghanistan.

organizations for vignette submission by email. The request for submissions occurred via email distribution lists and posts to organizations' Facebook groups. To enhance these submissions and ensure a larger sample set, point-to-point outreach was conducted, often via a snowball method of recommendations from interviewees.[4] We also worked with the sponsor to connect with DoD personnel (in particular, gender advisers [GENADs]) with potential vignettes for inclusion. Vignettes were collected via email from January 2022 to August 2022, and they were provided by DoD civilians, active-duty and reservist service members, and veterans. Follow-on interviews were conducted to obtain further vignette details as needed. All participants provided their verbal consent.

By speaking directly to GENADs and subject-matter experts across all the CCMDs and conducting a literature review, we were also able to identify areas of concern for WPS implementation in the DoD space. These insights clarify the current state of WPS and are presented in the conclusion.

Considerations

It is worth noting that within the literature regarding the inclusion of women in the military, there is a dichotomy between an emphasis on *gender neutrality*, which approaches inclusion as an issue of women's equality with men, and *gender differences*, which reasons that woman should be included because they contribute something unique to the force (Heinecken, 2017). There are concerns with both approaches: The first encourages women to conform to established masculine norms, while the latter encourages gender essential- ism.[5] These themes play out within the vignettes we present in this report. Although we endeavor to ensure that we are not perpetuating gender stereo- types, we do not attempt to adjust the perspectives shared with us.

Canadian Army Chief Warrant Officer Crystal Harris takes notes on integrating gender into military operations during the Operational Gender Advisor Course on December 6, 2018, hosted by U.S. Southern Command in Doral, Florida. The class of 20 military and civilians received joint credit for completing this five-day training course, which supports the mandate in the WPS Act of 2017 and the U.S. National Action Plan on WPS.

Why Do WPS and Gender Diversity Matter for DoD Operations, Activities, and Investments?

Local Manbij Military Council trainees learn marksmanship training on February 21, 2017, at Sanaa Training Center in Northwest Syria. The council is a multi-ethnic force that includes Kurds, Arabs, Christians, Turkmen, Yazidis, and others.

Studies suggest that across the conflict continuum, peace and security efforts are more likely to succeed when women play a role in them (Karim and Beardsley, 2017; Krause, Krause, and Bränfors, 2018). The DoD SFIP recognizes women's position in peace and security as service members, allies, peacebuilders, organizers, leaders, and advocates for their equal participation. However, in the United States and abroad, women face barriers that inhibit their ability to engage in these efforts, thereby handicapping international operations. Therefore, DoD operations, activities, and investments (OAIs) are limited when they do not incorporate gender perspectives. Additionally, understanding the operational environment from a gender perspective can help DoD identify how it can advance WPS within the conduct of its OAIs abroad whether it is cooperating, competing, or in conflict.

9

Cooperation

The National Security Strategy outlines two primary challenges facing the United States—strategic competition with Russia and China and transnational threats exacerbated by such things as climate change and global pandemics (White House, 2021; White House, 2022a; White House, 2022b). Transnational threats often contain gendered components and exacerbate existing gender inequalities around the world (Garamone, 2022). In the case of climate change, women in some countries may need to go further to get fresh water, increasing their risk of assault or kidnapping (Allen et al., 2020). Identifying where security threats exist and the gender dynamics at play can help the United States be more deliberate in its approach to partnership and outreach, by focusing on building individual and community resilience in vulnerable areas. Security cooperation OAIs to address these challenges will need to account for the ways in which such threats affect women and men differently (Prescott, 2014).

Integrating WPS principles into security cooperation activities can mitigate some of these challenges by ensuring women's meaningful participation in decisionmaking, empowering women in security sector roles, protecting vulnerable populations from violence, and providing for equitable access to resources. This integration is accomplished by bolstering partner capabilities and incorporating gender perspectives in training and exercises focused on confronting national security threats. Research shows that countries that subordinate women through inequitable laws, customs, and practices have higher likelihoods of corruption, violence, and instability (Hudson et al., 2020).

Furthermore, women are crucial to the successful transition to democracy and the successful maintenance of democratic society (Chenoweth and Marks, 2022). These factors suggest that promoting women's basic welfare contributes to more inclusion of women, which can ultimately lead to better democratic outcomes. Studies also show correlations between gender equality and likelihood of experiencing conflict—sustainable development and lower levels of interpersonal violence are seen in countries with higher levels of gender equality, suggesting reduced likelihood for conflict (Balon et al., 2016). Understanding these atmospheric data inform DoD decisionmakers on how to tailor their operational approach to a competition context; by understanding the dynamics at play, from a gender perspective, DoD can strategically choose how to strengthen its relationships with allies and cooperative partners.

Competition

Incorporating WPS principles as a component of strategic competition could facilitate a more holistic approach to preventing and deterring conflict. The United States can bolster its goal to be a preferred partner of choice with allies and partners by demonstrating a commitment to ensuring human rights and the rule of law. Such an approach provides strategic advantage over near-peer competitors who do not support the same rules-based international order. By exemplifying a diverse force through the meaningful employment of women in the joint force, the United States can foster external legitimacy and project influence with external audiences (Slapakova et al., 2022). By contrast, near-peer competitors, such as China and Russia, pursue patriarchal authoritarianism that promotes traditional gender roles and often excludes women, which may be at odds with the normative views of other countries in their respective regions (Chenoweth and Marks, 2022).

DoD has highlighted specific activities that are likely to be included in competition below the threshold of conflict. These include intelligence activities, cyberspace operations, and activities in the information environment (Joint Doctrine Note 1-19, 2019). Ensuring diversity of lived experiences and backgrounds within military occupational specialties conducting these types of activities can strengthen operations by broadening what is considered. Including a gender perspective when examining the operational environment expands DoD's understanding of social, economic, political, and cultural dynamics. It also examines the ways in which equality and inequality may affect decisionmaking within a cultural context (Egnell, 2016). Weak political institutions enable environments where illicit activities may thrive, such as modern slavery and human trafficking.[6] Considering gender perspectives when identifying drivers of inequality and engaging partners to improve institutions can reduce their impact on vulnerable populations and highlight the disproportional impact that weak institutions have on women and children.

Conflict and Crisis

Women's experiences in and with conflict are diverse. In situations of war, women and girls are affected differently and, in some cases, more severely than men and boys. Often, women bear particular violence, especially as civilians are increasingly targeted by combatants (Balon et al., 2016). Recent research highlights that a third of recent conflicts included sexual exploitation and forced marriage and almost 17 percent included human trafficking, both elements of modern slavery (Datta, Smith, and Bales, 2022). Incorporating gender perspectives accounts for the differences to better meet the needs of everyone—men, women, and children—in conflict zones. We also note that women are not just the victims of conflict—they fulfill myriad roles, including as combatants. Assuming all women are noncombatants can have profound security implications, which can be detrimental to both men and women.

Women involved in the tactical, day-to-day roles of peacekeeping or fighting can often better work with civilian populations on the ground because of cultural norms, expectations, and requirements related to cultural gender sensitivities (Egnell, 2016). They may also notice different things in situational assessments. For example, female engagement teams deployed in Iraq and Afghanistan ensured better access to the entire population often resulting in increased situational awareness, information sharing, and intelligence gathering (McNierney, 2015).

Beyond major conflict, DoD OAIs will be conducted in regions facing crises that will call for humanitarian assistance and disaster relief, for example. Such activities must consider the differential needs of the civilian population to ensure women and other underrepresented communities have equal access to relief. For example, women and children may require different diets. They need safe facilities. To be able to attend informational sessions, women may need access to child care. By accounting for this in planning, DoD operations will go more smoothly, with fewer failures on the ground.

Incorporating WPS principles can also affect the success of end-stages of conflict. As the United States supports stabilization and reconstruction efforts globally, the inclusion of women in peace processes can lead to more-sustainable negotiated settlements (Chenoweth and Marks, 2022). When women are included in these processes, they often push for equitable economic opportunity and access to health care and education (O'Reilly, 2016). This factor has an impact on democratic transitions, making them more likely to occur.

Supporting WPS Principles and Defense Objectives: *Vignettes*

Navy LTJG Tamora Holland, a medical officer with the Paktika Provincial Reconstruction Team and female engagement team leader, is greeted by Alamina, a community development facilitator for Urgun, at the first women's shura (consultative gathering) at the Urgun hospital on April 25, 2011.

The vignettes in this section provide examples of how the joint force has incorporated WPS principles into operations to support the DoD objectives outlined in the SFIP. These are examples of successes in which WPS principles were recognized, accounted for, and implemented. Some of the vignettes identify areas where more could have been done to advance WPS principles. As we acknowledge earlier, these are by no means exhaustive and are context-specific. Many other instances of incorporating WPS principles to improve outcomes for women and children and for national security as a whole certainly exist.

For each vignette, we indicate which DoD WPS objectives were met.

 Defense objective 1

 Defense objective 2

 Defense objective 3

The Role of Women in U.S.–Joint Forces in Afghanistan

Ktah Khas Afghan FTP members participate in morning physical training outside Kabul, Afghanistan. The women work closely alongside the men on operations to engage and interact with other women and children.

In 2014, the United States officially ended combat operations in Afghanistan and committed to pulling out U.S. troops by the end of 2016.[7] However, the United States continued to train, advise, and assist Afghan forces under the NATO Resolute Support Mission (RSM). As part of RSM, NATO was authorized to conduct special operations activities in support of the Afghan special operations forces (SOF). Although most Afghan SOF missions were conducted independently, U.S. SOF provided critical enabling capabilities that were lacking within Afghan SOF, such as planning, advising, and intelligence support (Central Command [CENTCOM], 2016).[8] U.S. Air Force Special Operations Command (AFSOC) deployed U-28 aircraft to Afghanistan to assist with the intelligence, surveillance, and reconnaissance (ISR) capabilities required to support Afghan SOF.

AFSOC pilots and combat systems officers (CSOs) provided combat sensing capabilities to operations in Afghanistan, as mission critical leaders and the "eyes and ears" of their fellow airmen. To ensure operational effectiveness, there needs to be clear communication and a shared understanding of the battlefield between air and ground forces. Trust is essential in executing these types of missions given how quickly the situation changes and decisions are made.

These AFSOC units were gender integrated for both pilots and CSOs. Because of the deployment of Afghan women as SOF operators, having gender integrated units both in the air and on the ground enhanced sensing operations leading to critical intelligence gains.

Provincial Reconstruction Team members traveled to the Panjshir Valley on December 17, 2009, to meet with Afghan women in the area. Service members deployed to Forward Operating Base Lion to work hand-in-hand with the local Afghan women, teaching them such things as first aid and how to increase their crop output.

*1st Lt Emily Chilson
interacts with the
girls in Urgun,
Afghanistan, during
the first women's
shura on April 25,
2011.*

How WPS Principles Were Applied or Implemented

During mission planning stages, the presence of Afghan SOF women proved key to gaining intelligence for sensing missions. These forces gathered information from women and children in ways Afghan men and foreign SOF were not able to. Per Afghan cultural norms, male soldiers cannot talk to Afghan women and their children; female AFSOC members could speak to Afghan women and children but required an interpreter, making it difficult to pick up on cultural nuances. Because Afghan SOF women were fluent in the language and aware of local customs, they were able to engage with women and children in a culturally acceptable way, making those they interacted with more comfortable and forthcoming with information. Additionally, because of the restrictive nature of RSM, U.S. forces were limited in their ability to operate with "boots on the ground." Afghan SOF women were able to fill the gap in capability.

With respect to the airborne ISR missions, Afghan SOF operators who were women were able to identify and access areas for conducting sensing operations in areas where AFSOC had previously not focused. As one AFSOC CSO stated, "So much of the intel was focused on following the guys. . . . They [the Afghan SOF operators who were women] would know where certain doors that accessed women's quarters were to the building and how to access those." The Afghan SOF women knew what areas of living compounds were designated for women and children and communicated that to airborne assets, providing crucial information for the operation. As summarized by the AFSOC

CSO, "Context is the biggest thing they gave. We didn't go in with context and were trying to retroactively apply it."

The inclusion of airmen who are women in operations also demonstrated the joint force's commitment to leading by example. Despite language barriers, seeing American counterparts leading missions increased the confidence of the Afghan operators that women can execute these operations, according to the AFSOC CSO. Initially while operating, Afghan SOF women were surprised to hear other women on the radio and even had their own doubts about their American counterparts' abilities. However, U.S. AFSOC CSOs who were women quickly proved themselves to be essential. And Afghan SOF women began specifically requesting to work with U.S. AFSOC women by callsign. The airman we interviewed said she felt that there was an innate understanding between CSOs who were women and Afghan SOF women that connected them. From her perspective, this implicit knowledge and shared context made executing operations much smoother.

Operational Impact and Broader Observations

The importance of enabling women in partner nations to meaningfully partici-pate and serve across defense and security sectors is evident in how AFSOC ISR missions in Afghanistan were strengthened by the role of Afghan SOF women. Likewise, having women within special operations squadrons con-ducting airborne ISR—a core mission of AFSOC—provided important context to sensing missions and enabled critical partnerships with Afghan SOF women on the ground.

Integrating Women into the Guyanese Defense Forces

Members of the Guyana Defence Force (GDF) participate in a foot patrol during the Tradewinds 2021 training exercise at Camp Seweyo, Co-operative Republic of Guyana, on June 22, 2021.

Every year, U.S. Southern Command (SOUTHCOM) sponsors a joint exercise with partner nations in the Caribbean (known as Tradewinds) aimed at increasing the capacity to collaboratively conduct humanitarian assistance/disaster relief operations and counter transnational organized crime.[9] About 1,500 U.S. military, partner nation security, and civilian personnel—including U.S. forces and U.S. government agencies, the nations of the Caribbean Community, and such regional agencies as the Regional Security System, the Implementation Agency for Crime and Security, and the Caribbean Disaster Emergency Management Agency—participated in the exercise, which was hosted by Guyana (SOUTHCOM, undated). In 2021, for the first time since these exercises began in the 1980s, the United States and its partners began incorporating a gender perspective in the Tradewinds exercise.

How WPS Principles Were Applied and Implemented

The integration of WPS principles into the 2021 Tradewinds exercise had two key components: an academic training component and a practical exercise component. For the academic training portion, military and law enforcement personnel from partner countries had the opportunity to take part in courses on the importance of promoting and integrating women in the defense and security sectors. These courses were tailored by career field (e.g., police, border security) allowing for a more nuanced exploration of gender-related challenges and tools specific to different functions. In addition, courses were tailored to different domains. With the maritime domain training, instructors discussed human trafficking on cruise ships; for the jungle training, instructors talked about things that can happen in that domain—not only combat and crisis but also how to react when women are on teams: How do you treat them? What are the accommodations (e.g., will they have separate tents or not, where will they use the restroom)? How do you maintain professional relationships?

For the practical exercise portion, SOUTHCOM GENADs sought to integrate the principles of WPS in specific scenarios that were part of the Tradewinds exercise. One scenario involved a simulation of a human trafficking event. As part of the scenario, participants learned how to conduct a gender analysis when scanning physical environments for potential threats. Adding a gender lens encourages participants to consider the different interactions between men and women in the environment—how they are behaving, what is influencing their decisions—and how men and women are differently perceiving and being perceived as threats. For example, if a restaurant is being assessed, security personnel may ask why there are no women. And if women

Soldiers with the Army National Guard's 2-54th Security Force Assistance Brigade depart for the Tradewinds 2021 training exercise.

are there, what state or condition are they in? How many of them are there in comparison with men? Being able to quickly identify the relative number of men and women in a room, for example, can provide helpful information that may lead to more-effective risk assessments and responses. Importantly, though, a gender lens does not simply mean pay attention to women as victims. SOUTHCOM GENADs emphasized that they intentionally designed the groups of victims and perpetrators to include both men and women to highlight to participants that individuals involved in trafficking may defy established gender norms and expectations. "To assume that when you see a group of women, they are all victims is an operational mistake," said one adviser involved in designing the training.[10]

Interestingly, the WPS training component led to broader discussions about the barriers to incorporating women in operational roles among partner defense forces, which led to changes in the GDF. Historically, the Western and resource-rich portion of Guyana—known as the Essequibo—has been hotly contested between Venezuela and Guyana. In recent years, tensions between the two South American nations have escalated with the discovery of oil in the Essequibo in 2015 and Venezuela's worsening social and economic crisis, which has resulted in an influx of Venezuelan refugees into Guyana and other neighboring countries, a situation that has been exploited by human traffickers (Angelo, 2022; U.S. Department of State, undated-a). At the time of the 2021 Tradewinds exercise, the GDF was experiencing a shortage in security personnel at the border.

When leading one of the WPS classes, SOUTH-COM GENADs noticed that most of the Guyanese women in uniform were performing support functions, such as serving food in the dining facilities. When they followed up, the advisers learned that some of these women had received operational training and were prepared to deploy to the border between Guyana and Venezuela, seen as a premier mission within the GDF. However, women serving in the GDF who would have sought to participate in the border mission were precluded from doing so by a lack of facilities, including dormitories and restrooms. Given traditional cultural norms regarding gender roles in Guyana, facilities for women in operational deployments were likely an afterthought for GDF planners. The SOUTHCOM GENADs reached out to the U.S. Security Cooperation Office (SCO) in Guyana, which then worked with the GDF to set up separate women's facilities at the border. In October 2021, the first group of GDF women were deployed to the Guyana side of the border. Seven months later, a second group of women were deployed to the Venezuelan side of the border. "This is an example of how sharing an idea through training can lead to the operationalization of the role of women," said a SOUTHCOM representative.[11] Although women have always worked alongside operations units as enablers—for example, in technical supporting roles, such as translators, medics, and intelligence analysts—the case with the GDF shows how removing structural barriers that prohibit meaningful gender participation allows for the greater integration of women into operational units and contributes to Guyana's force strength.

For us, it was a no-brainer—on one hand, you had a manpower shortage, on the other hand, you had enthusiastic women ready to deploy. So, we elevated the issue and worked with the SCO. A month later, at an after-action meeting—the SCO (our liaison in the embassy) let us know that the first group of women were sent in October of last year to the border.

—SOUTHCOM GENAD

Operational Impact and Broader Observations

By bringing WPS principles and experts to bear on the 2021 Tradewinds exercise, Guyana was able to address an operational obstacle and the United States gained a partner in the SOUTHCOM region that has men and women in uniform who are better equipped to detect the nuances and dynamics of challenges, such as human trafficking, enhancing the security and stability of nations across the region.

21

Evacuating Female Tactical Platoon Members

Paratroopers assigned to the 1st Brigade Combat Team, 82nd Airborne
Division, based out of Fort Bragg, North Carolina, facilitate the safe
evacuation of U.S. citizens, Special Immigrant Visa applicants, and other
at-risk Afghans out of Afghanistan as quickly and safely as possible from
Hamid Karzai International Airport in Kabul on August 22, 2021.

Beginning in 2010, the U.S. special operations community began training women military members without special operations training to become part of cultural support teams (CSTs) (Tracy, 2016).[12] Until the end of U.S. combat operations in Afghanistan in 2014, CSTs provided support to U.S. SOF teams engaging with civilian Afghan women and women in the Afghan SOF, which male SOF team members previously were unable to do due to cultural differences (Katt, 2014). CSTs are often highlighted as an example of WPS principles in practice within the U.S. military, while also supporting the inclusion of Afghan women into their country's security forces. When U.S. and coalition forces prepared to leave Afghanistan, CST members were at the forefront of working to ensure that their peers in the Afghan SOF were not left in danger.

How WPS Principles Were Applied or Implemented

The CST program graduated over 250 American women, representing a small community that has remained in contact over the past decade. The majority of CST members supported the U.S. SOF teams during village stability operations and direct-action operations. However, a small number of CSTs trained Afghan women who were members of the Female Tactical Platoon (FTP) (Ripley, 2022). Because of the general cultural limitations on positions and jobs that Afghan women could fill, U.S. and Afghan security officials limited publicizing the FTP's role. Moreover, Afghan platoon members themselves were reluctant to publicize their role, concerned about their and their families' security in the event their jobs was known: "When I was in country, they were hesitant to have their pictures taken because they were afraid neighbors would find out," according to a CST alumna. In the years prior to the withdrawal from Afghanistan, CST members among themselves discussed the risks and dangers their trainees would face and what they could do to help FTP members.

We had been saying for years when the United States pulls out, it will be extremely dangerous for these women. . . . A few years before the pull out started, we started to talk about what to do about it.

In the weeks immediately preceding the U.S. withdrawal, as the Taliban began to take over more territory in Afghanistan, CST alumnae began coalescing in a private Facebook group to figure out how to help FTP members trying to depart Afghanistan. By the time Kabul fell on August 15, 2021, CST alumnae—a mix of active duty, reservist, and retired U.S. military women—

FTP members fire on a range during a qualification exercise on March 13, 2018, near Kabul, Afghanistan.

were actively coordinating between themselves and FTP members to aid their transit to Hamid Karzai International Airport (HKIA) in Kabul to be evacuated.

Evacuation efforts were compromised not only by the Taliban but also by U.S. evacuation criteria. With respect to the former, the Taliban allowed families to pass through security only if a man was a U.S. passport holder, reflecting local patriarchal norms. Moreover, men generally had freedom of movement, where individual FTP members did not. Additionally, many of the FTP members were responsible for younger siblings or family members who did not meet evacuation criteria established by the United States, forcing difficult decisions among families.

Notwithstanding these challenges, former CST members leveraged their networks to ensure that FTP members were admitted into HKIA. Through a maze of unofficial contacts, CST alumnae were able to link FTP women with specific gate guards to gain access. "We also sent a letter to the women on the ground." The letter was a copy of an August 16, 2021, letter to Secretary of State Antony Blinken and Secretary of Homeland Security Alejandro Mayorkas, signed by 46 U.S. Senators. It specifically named the FTP, among other categories of Afghan women, as being at particular risk from the Taliban and requiring relocation to the United States (U.S. Senate, 2021).

> If they were able to get close to the airport, they were able to show the letter to security and were able to get to the gate. Having that letter aided in the split-second decision of whether to let them on the plane or not.[13]

> Ultimately, according to the CST alumna, the CST network was able to assist 40 FTP members in their evacuation from Afghanistan before the U.S. officially withdrew; an additional 20 platoon members remain in Afghanistan as of summer 2022.

Operational Impact and Broader Observations

Although the CST and FTP programs leveraged the skills and access of both American and Afghan women security force members while the programs existed, the relationships endured beyond training and operations. The bonds built between women soldiers empowered them and emphasized the critical role they played in Afghanistan's security, not unlike the bond between many male U.S. service members and Afghan interpreters or service members. One notable difference between men's and women's experiences during the evacuation was evident in U.S. policy that primarily provided Special Immigration Visas (SIVs) for male Afghan security force members while working to secure their evacuation, making the success of CST members in evacuating their counterparts all the more admirable. Moreover, FTP members are in "the middle of a Venn diagram between vulnerable identities," which include gender, ethnicity, and supporters of U.S. and coalition forces. "When they get talked about its as women, but this doesn't capture the whole picture. There are groups advocating for Afghan women. Groups that advocate for Afghan special operations members," but FTP members often fall through the cracks because they do not neatly fit into one category, according to the CST alumna.

Leveraging Partnerships and Data to Meet Strategic Objectives in the U.S. Indo-Pacific Command

*An Indonesian army soldier and Philippine army
soldier, students during the WPS initiatives
and integration into peacekeeping operations,
answer questions during a class at Pusat Misi
Pemeliharaan, Indonesia, on July 19, 2022.*

In 2020, U.S. Indo-Pacific Command (INDOPACOM) GENADs identified a data gap in their partner nation engagements.[14] Although they were able to engage with local U.S. embassies and hear about examples of gender-based issues in the region, the INDOPACOM GENADs sought more-concrete data that backed up these firsthand accounts for senior leaders. INDOPACOM began working with the Pacific Disaster Center (PDC)—an applied science, information, and technology center managed by the University of Hawaii that focuses on reducing disaster risks—to use data to understand the drivers of gender inequality and enhance DoD's ability to invest in long-term programs that improve gender-based resilience, peace, and security in the Asia-Pacific region. GENADs we spoke with reported that although data analytics has become a popular topic within DoD, the systematic use of gender data analytics has not been fully realized across the CCMDs to inform policy decisions. PDC offers a unique opportunity to bridge this gap in the WPS space. "PDC's data analysis provides a baseline for measuring progress toward INDOPACOM's strategic objectives in our area of responsibility," said one GENAD. "This encourages us to take ownership of our programs and helps keep us accountable."[15]

How WPS Principles Were Applied and Implemented

Beginning in 2021, in partnership with INDOPACOM, PDC has maintained a comparative, cross-country index for WPS responsiveness that includes measures of both gender empowerment and inequality (e.g., the ratio of male-to-female employers, number of women in law enforcement, access to prenatal care, and the male-to-female adult literacy ratio) and threats that are of strategic importance to DoD and can negatively impact women's participation, inclusion, and integration in a given society (e.g., conflict, non-state malign actors, climate change, and maritime security). Although drivers of gender inequality have not been as emphasized as other factors when designing security cooperation assistance, DoD is increasingly recognizing the importance of taking a more holistic view of potential threats to stability and security among its partner nations (White House, 2021; White House, 2022a; White House, 2022b). Analysts highlighted that many indicators are cross-cutting and can point to a nation's resiliency and responsiveness, even if they do not appear to have gender components.

Since its creation in 2021, the WPS responsiveness index has been used by the INDOPACOM commander to help establish priorities for engagement efforts with partner nations in the Asia-Pacific region. When programs or activities are considered, the responsiveness index provides an indication of what that country's resiliency level may be and if certain activities might improve

*What makes the WPS
responsiveness score
different from other
indices is the exposure
component. What are
the driving factors in a
given country that could
be sources of instability?
Everything from malign
actors to natural
disasters.*

—PDC ANALYST

their stability. For example, in Timor-Leste, a young democracy in southeast Asia that is strategically important to the United States, DoD and State Department officials identified human trafficking as a critical concern based on the responsiveness index.[16] Specifically, poor economic conditions and limited educational opportunities in Timor-Leste create trafficking vulnerabilities for Timorese nationals, particularly women and girls. In August 2021, in partnership with the International Organization for Migration, INDOPACOM sponsored a two-day Combating Trafficking in Persons workshop for Timor-Leste labor inspectors. This was the first time the country convened labor inspectors for a training of this kind. The training focused on victim identification, victim referral, and working with agencies outside the labor department, such as with law enforcement.

INDOPACOM GENADs observed that the training positively impacted Timor-Leste's annual rating for the State Department's Trafficking in Persons (TIP) Report, which ranks governments based on their perceived efforts to acknowledge and combat human trafficking. Failure to meet the minimum TIP rating can negatively affect a country's ability to access U.S. foreign assistance, making the TIP scores particularly important for low-income countries, such as Timor-Leste. GENADs also emphasized that in the long term, addressing human trafficking in Timor-Leste will help contribute to a more stable regional partner.

In another example, INDOPACOM GENADs identified the Pacific Islands nations as a gender inequality "hotspot," given that many of these countries ranked lowest on the PDC WPS responsiveness index for gender equality and empowerment while also being highly susceptible to risks related to climate change. To better understand the dynamics between the responsiveness scores for gender equality and climate change, INDOPACOM partnered with Center for Naval Analyses and civil society organizations to host a series of workshops on climate security with Pacific Islander women in November 2020 and December 2020. During these workshops, INDOPACOM GENADs learned that for many of the women, climate change is intrinsically linked to gender-based violence. For example, changes in the climate may force women and girls to walk far to collect drinking water, which increases their risk of being assaulted. INDOPACOM representatives explained that although the United States is interested in working with Pacific Island nations for "strategic com-

petition," failing to hear the voices of women will inevitably lead to gaps in security cooperation activities: "We will never have a stable partner unless we address gender-based violence—until we address that, we're not going to get to sustained outcomes. The gender perspective is a pathway to representative democracy, and democracy is a powerful weapon against competitors."[17] Using the PDC data to highlight gender-based issues enables INDOPACOM to recognize and address issues not traditionally recognized by security sectors but critical to their success.

Operational Impact and Broader Observations

PDC and INDOPACOM representatives stressed that there is a strategic advantage associated with taking a broader social and cultural approach to assessing security risks and building partnerships in the Asia-Pacific region. They pointed specifically to China, which has focused almost exclusively on providing economic assistance through large infrastructure projects that may not necessarily align with the country's immediate needs and vulnerabilities. "Applying a gender lens to analyzing and implementing regional partnerships provides us with an unmatched competitive advantage,"[18] said one INDOPA-COM GENAD. By working with partner nations to address these diverse sources of insecurity, the United States can make those countries stronger and more resilient, thus supporting U.S. defense objectives. PDC representatives also emphasized that from a security standpoint, where you leave gaps, you leave opportunities for competitors to come in and fill those gaps.

A child from a school in Baucau, Timor-Leste, poses for a photo during a site survey at the school on September 9, 2022. The operation focused on capacity-building through health services outreach, engineering civic action program construction projects, and subject-matter expert exchanges.

Protecting Vulnerable Populations and Ensuring Equitable Access to Information and Services for Refugees

A child smiles as she awaits to board her flight during an evacuation on August 21, 2021, at Hamid Karzai International Airport, in Kabul, Afghanistan.

As U.S. military operations in Afghanistan drew to a close in August 2021, the U.S. government worked to expedite the evacuation of tens of thousands of Afghans, including SIV holders and applicants, resulting in a flood of evacuees requiring resettlement assistance in the United States.[19] On August 29, 2021, President Joseph Biden tasked the U.S. Department of Homeland Security (DHS) with providing temporary housing, sustainment, and support for evacuees (DHS, undated). Requiring a whole-of-government approach to the mission, DHS coordinated with other government agencies to provide capability support that was not inherent to their department. Under the Homeland Defense and Defense Support of Civil Authorities (DSCA) mission, DoD, through U.S. Northern Command (NORTHCOM), was approved to provide the evacuees housing, sustainment, and other support within the United States.

This effort, known as Operation Allies Welcome (OAW), marked the first time that DoD deployed its GENAD workforce as a capability to address gender dynamics within a current military operation.

How WPS Was Applied and Implemented

During initial planning for OAW, GENADs both within the Office of the Secretary of Defense (OSD) and NORTHCOM identified a need to holistically consider WPS principles in DoD's approach to evacuation and resettlement services, as they were not considered systematically, if at all. Incorporating gender perspectives into the mission included applying WPS principles, such as women's inclusion and participation, equitable access, and prevention and protection from violence in task force operations and processes. However, during early stages of the operation, senior military officials did not immediately recognize the relevance and/or necessity of this approach to achieve operational objectives because this was the first time these perspectives had been incorporated in a DSCA mission. Some officials worried that GENADs might act as some kind of "gender correctness police," issuing reports on how the task forces were or were not doing on gender considerations, rather than understanding the potential operational impact.

Evacuation operations could have benefited from a consideration of gender factors in the earlier phases. A primary planning assumption was that a majority of Afghans evacuating would be military age men brought in as SIVs. Because of the expedited manner of the evacuation, SIVs were accompanied by a significant population of family groups comprising of women, children, and elderly. Hence, contracts for family housing, medical needs for a diverse population, behavioral health needs, and child nutrition had not been considered or budgeted. When it came to nutrition, beverage options included soda and

Capt. Emily Copple leads the Operation Allies Welcome Female Engagement Team on September 14, 2021. The team ensures a soldier presence at the temporary housing facilities at Rhine Ordnance Barracks and Ramstein Air Force Base in Germany for Afghan travelers at all times, helping to bridge cultural gaps and provide a supportive environment for men and women.

other items that were not appropriate for small children, while excluding such items as formula. As for medical needs, adequate women's health resources (in particular, obstetrics) were not factored in and had to be rapidly provided. Moreover, inadequate numbers of providers and interpreters who are women were available, critical for the religious and cultural considerations of the population. When these challenges were identified, solutions were considered in silos, rather than holistically and as interrelated problems. In response, OSD and NORTHCOM GENADs made a compelling case for taking a comprehensive approach to consider gender dimensions for all aspects of the mission. This response resulted in the inclusion of GENADs at all the task forces.

Once GENADs were in place, they served as effective communicators between DoD, interagency, and nongovernmental organization (NGO) personnel to incorporate relevant gender-based information and assistance into the mission. Applying WPS principles resulted in three primary impacts: protection of women and children, equitable access to resources and services, and equitable access to information.

As one GENAD noted, "When you are bringing in people to live in a camp environment, there are gender-based risks to the transient and group setting." Therefore, *protection* for all evacuees, especially women and children, was a key priority. During site surveys, GENADs highlighted the need to assess the adequacy of lighting, identify appropriate locations of latrines for women

and girls, and determine different housing options based on family needs, all of which led to safer living conditions for the entire population. Additionally, GENADs advocated to support potential victims of gender-based violence. This work required a specific understanding of sensitivities related to gender-based violence response in a refugee environment. For instance, many of the women and children at the task force locations were there because of their husband's or another male relative's SIV status. In such cases, women may be hesitant to report instances of gender-based violence if they thought it might jeopardize their ability to remain in the United States. To standardize the response to gender-based violence across the task forces, DHS and State Department established a gender-vulnerable population protection advisory group, supported by DoD. The group developed standard operating procedures for gender-based violence response at each of the task forces and addressed sensitivities, such as who had access to reports and ensuring responses were survivor-based.

In addition to protection, the inclusion of GENADs into OAW helped provide *equitable access to resources and services*. At first, much of the task force programing was centered on a gender-neutral experience that did not account for the differing needs of the population. This made it challenging for women to access resources and services in the same way as men. For example, at first, access to the supply store where evacuees were able to purchase

Morgan Gwinn, Department of Defense Education Activity teacher and USO volunteer, shows the child care supplies storage area on September 3, 2021, at the USO-Kaiserslautern in the Joint Mobility Processing Center, Ramstein Air Base, Germany during Operation Allies Refuge. The USO team and volunteers welcomed the evacuees off the planes and gave them supplies and food.

33

necessary items was equal in the amount of time allowed. However, men usually shopped alone whereas women often shopped with children and were purchasing items for the entire family. GENADs helped the command understand that the goal should be equitable—rather than simply equal—access to resources. Therefore, women were allotted more time in the store to account for these gendered differences.

Third, the inclusion of a gendered perspective promoted *equitable access to information*. It was important to understand how information was being passed, who was potentially not receiving the information, and what could be done to ensure that all members of the population had equitable access to information. Initially, information was primarily put on boards in common areas, but not all the population was literate, so finding other ways to pass information was vital. Most of the task forces held town hall meetings, but attendees were primarily men as women either lacked child care or they were expected to not attend activities where men and women mixed and were therefore dependent on men for information. Additionally, task forces needed to consider what information women may uniquely require, such as gender-based violence reporting and evacuation status particulars. GENADs advocated for women-only town halls because as one GENAD explained, "getting information to women was so important and so we had to be deliberate." Identifying these barriers helped task force personnel ensure that women-centered programing was offered in a culturally sensitive manner to encourage the full participation of women.

Operational Impact and Broader Observations

Beyond the direct impact that applying WPS principles had on women and children in task force locations, OAW was a successful proof of concept that demonstrates the utility of applying such an approach in DSCA and other operations, such as disaster relief. Notwithstanding these successes, there were several challenges that provided lessons for future undertakings. For example, because of senior officials' concerns about "gender correctness policing," the integration of the GENADs was restricted so that reporting related to gender considerations remained internal to the assigned task force. This constrained the ability of GENADs to communicate and network, which could have been a force multiplier.

Another challenge that limited WPS implementation within the task force was the limited availability of GENADs, which made it difficult to provide sustained gender advisory support to each of the task forces. Some organizations were hesitant to give up personnel for operational support, others could only send personnel for a limited time. Furthermore, the over-reliance on contractors in the WPS space within DoD led to additional bureaucratic hurdles that had to be overcome as the task forces could not do a request for forces for

35

external support. To mitigate these challenges, NORTHCOM devised an adaptive approach to GENAD support based on the task force's needs.

Finally, in the future, incorporation of WPS principles in resettlement efforts, or even broader humanitarian assistance/disaster relief operations, should be incorporated from the start. In the case of OAW, had GENADs been included in the initial phase, the approach to infrastructure creation could have been more intentional and resulted in different installation layouts, security considerations, design of lineups for the dining facilities, and other critical aspects of infrastructure design that would have ensured the equitable access to facilities and information and ensured the safety of all vulnerable populations.

A U.S. service member high-fives a child who was evacuated from Afghanistan on August 21, 2021, at Al Udeid Air Base, Qatar.

Additional Insights

Surrounded by the bright aura of the National Security Agency's cutting-edge Cybersecurity Collaboration Center, women from across the country recently joined leaders from U.S. Cyber Command and the National Security Agency on August 2, 2022, to learn about the agency's mission and to shine a light on the future of cybersecurity.

During our interviews, we collected numerous insights into other areas where the application of WPS principles is being developed. These lessons reflect other efforts to incorporate WPS principles into DoD activities and operations.

Women Can Play a Critical Role in Social Engineering and Cybersecurity

As DoD works to incorporate WPS principles across various military occupational specialties, discussions with officials singled out a desire to better understand how gender approaches to cyber operations may be considered. Available research clearly points to the significance of gender in social engineering. For example, participants of a 2021 study of the attributes that social engineers ascribe to successful deceptions recounted conforming to stereotypes surrounding their age, race, and accents to play on the biases of a targeted individual (Steinmetz, 2021).

Reinforcing this finding, during the social engineering competition at the fifth annual Def Con—the world's largest hacker convention—women significantly outcompeted men in gathering protected information from targeted companies (Eddy, 2013). Although the reasons for this gap are not completely clear, contestants' pretexts for contacting companies did exhibit some noticeable differences along gender lines. Specifically, most participants who are women portrayed themselves as not being technically savvy (i.e., "damsel in distress" trope) and asked for assistance from "fellow" employees when contacting company representatives, while male participants tended to pose as tech experts and, in some cases, even as CEOs. The women were significantly more successful in obtaining protected information.

An Air Force cybersecurity officer we interviewed underscored that this is a pattern she had seem play out repeatedly in the field.

> A woman will call up an IT department and say she has been locked out of her account. There may even be a recording of a baby crying in the background. She ends up getting her password changed and, from there, is able to access all types of secure information. This information can be used to steal identities or gain access to classified systems, ultimately feeding into higher-level operations.[20]

37

Former Prime Minister of Iran Mir Hossein Mousavi and his wife, Zahra Rahnavard, on election day of the 2009 Iranian presidential election.

Even with the proliferation of information technology, which has enabled the use of fabricated online personas, female personas controlled by women operatives tend to be much more convincing, according to this officer. Should the person be posing with a pet? Should there be a photo of that person with family? These are all factors that contribute directly to the believability of an online profile and, ultimately, may be critical to the success of an operation. Having a diversity of lived experiences and backgrounds within the cyber community might strengthen social engineering operations and broaden impact.

Failure to Understand Women's Roles in Society Can Affect Security Outcomes

In 2009, after irregularities in the Iranian presidential election led to widespread protests throughout the country (i.e., the Green Revolution), there was significant debate within the U.S. Intelligence Community about the goals and motivations of the protest movement.[21] It was unclear, for example, whether the Green Revolution was a popular denunciation of Iran's Islamic regime or a more-targeted protest of the election's obvious corruption. As a result of this debate, the U.S. government struggled to identify an appropriate response. One of the reasons for the disconnect was that while intelligence analysts spent lot of time understanding the presidential candidates, they generally ignored the candidates' significant relationships and influences outside the political and public sphere. A former civilian defense intelligence officer with experience in the CENTCOM area of operations with whom we spoke noted that one such person not on intelligence analysts' radar was reform-ist candidate Mir Hossein Mousavi's wife, Zahra Rahnavard, a renowned and charismatic scholar and Islamic feminist thinker with a large following of her own. "There is a bias that Americans have against Iran—they think of Iran as a conservative, Muslim country and fail to appreciate Iranian feminism," said the intelligence officer. Iran's women's rights movement was among the earliest in the world, and Iranian women have fought vigorously in the decades that fol-lowed the 1979 Islamic Revolution to regain the rights they lost after the fall of the Shah. "Rahnavard was a huge intellectual part of the Green Revolution and was even more popular than her husband. Most American watchers didn't pick up on that. If we had applied a gender perspective, maybe the U.S. could have engaged more constructively with the movement." Of note, the deaths of two protestors, Neda Agha-Soltan in the 2009 Green Revolution and Masha Amini in 2022, ignited significant protests and social unrest in Iran, highlighting the role of Iranian women in fighting for human and political rights (Fathi, 2009; Filkins, 2022; Peterson, 2022).

Inclusion of Men and Women in Diverse Roles Facilitates Problem-Solving Required for Complex Security Situations

Beginning in 2013, fighting throughout northeastern Syria, including within Raqqa, had already been heavy resulting in a widespread humanitarian crisis: between April 2017 and October 2017, nearly 270,000 civilians fled Raqqa and many would return to a significantly destroyed city (United Nations High Commissioner for Refugees, 2017).[22] Given the importance of stabilization and reconstruction, Special Operations Joint Task Force Operation-Inherent Resolve (SOJTF-OIR) understood that humanitarian assistance would require a whole-of-government approach, involving DoD, the State Department, and NGOs. However, little was being done to promote this coordination. One junior male officer recognized the problem but had little traction bringing people together. The senior SOF officer who eventually was brought in to coordinate the effort, a woman, told us that in her previous position in Pakistan, she was often tasked with building diplomatic and interagency partnerships. She noted that counterparts in the interagency, aid, and development spaces were also women, and that her command felt that as a woman she may be seen as less threatening and more empathetic than her male SOF counterparts and would therefore more easily achieve buy-in from these organizations. Whether that was true, these interactions helped the officer gain critical perspective on the organizational culture of groups external to the military—bridging some of the civil-military divide that can arise during operations with multiple stakeholders. "You can't try on empathy like a jacket at Nordstrom's; it has to be practiced," she said.

In this example, the traditional segregation of women into more "feminine" jobs led to a situation in which men in the SOJTF-OIR command did not have appropriate awareness of the issue that was necessary to address a critical problem. Without an effort to integrate both women *and* men into all roles across DoD, the military will not be able to meet the security situations of today and tomorrow that will require people to unpack complexity and solve problems not as a leader in isolation but cooperatively.

Targeted Gender Advisory Work Can Have Spillover Effects

In 2021, one junior officer we spoke with developed training courses to inform Civil Affairs personnel of the dangers of human trafficking and how to recognize such behavior.[23] Although not an official GENAD, based on her undergraduate education and interest in WPS, this officer identified a gap in DoD-provided training surrounding modern slavery and human trafficking, which was especially important for Civil Affairs personnel who have a unique role and access in partner countries. In collaboration with the University of Nottingham's Rights Lab (University of Nottingham, undated) and the Pacific Disaster Center, an introductory course was designed to discuss how human trafficking contributes to a country's lack of resiliency and potential for violent conflict and supports malign actors and criminal organizations.[24]

Civil Affairs professionals are specifically trained and educated to understand and work with the civil sector across the spectrum of conflict: from prevention of hostilities to assisting people in returning to daily life after hostilities or humanitarian crises end. Through the course, personnel become better equipped to understand the operating environment and avoid unintentionally supporting organizations utilizing any form of human trafficking and can properly report instances of these crimes without increasing harm to victims and risk to mission. In 2022, this introductory course was expanded to provide CCMD-specific training for deploying teams. Moreover, the trainings will be required for the Army's entire special operations community, which will improve mission success.

Women-Led Organizations Can Act as Important Intermediaries to Address Security Concerns

As a response to the Libyan Civil War in 2011, the United States and NATO undertook military operations (Operation Odyssey Dawn) to protect the civilian population (NATO, 2015).[25] At the same time, the African Union (AU) was the lead on pursuing a negotiated initiative to peacefully transition to a post-Qadhafi Libya—however, that effort was ultimately unsuccessful (Dewaal, 2012). The military success of Operation Odyssey Dawn but the diplomatic failure of the AU led to strained relations between the AU and the United States and NATO.

In the following years, American and NATO organizations, in particular, Allied Joint Force Command (JFC) Naples and the NATO Strategic Direction

South Hub (NSD-Hub),[26] looked for opportunities to improve their relationship with the AU. One such opportunity arose in 2019, as destabilizing factors on the African continent were having spillover effects onto the European continent. The Commander of JFC Naples along with the NATO Secretary General's Special Representative for Women, Peace and Security understood the importance of including women's perspectives in negotiations and coalition building. Therefore, JFC-Naples conducted outreach to women-led organizations on the African continent to build those relationships. Thus began an enduring partnership between JFC Naples, the NSD-Hub, and FemWise, an AU-affiliated organization of African women who work in conflict prevention and mediation.

This partnership has hosted multiple workshops and conferences on such topics as empowering women in leadership to improve stability and preventing and responding to conflict-related sexual violence. These workshops take a gender-focused approach to NATO operations by preventing gender-based violence and ensuring the meaningful participation of women in peace and security efforts. Additionally, the enduring relationship developed between FemWise and key NATO and U.S. organizations has helped strengthen the overall relationship with the AU.

Small groups discuss opportunities and challenges of women's integration in Burkina Faso. U.S. military personnel and Burkinabe leaders participate in the Women's Peace and Security Symposium on July 13, 2022, in Ouagadougou, Burkina Faso.

41

Conclusions

*U.S. Marines with Marine
Aircraft Control Group 18
listen to Col Lorna Mahlock,
commanding officer, MACG-18,
during Exercise Valiant Shield 16,
on September 14, 2016.*

As discussed throughout this report, WPS is a critical enabler for the U.S. military—for both internal operations and interactions with our partners and allies. In the years since the passage of the 2017 WPS Act, the global operating environment has changed from one focused on counterterrorism and counterinsurgency operations to one that prioritizes strategic competition and an increased emphasis on influence. Our vignettes and anecdotes provide examples of how to leverage WPS principles to support allies and partners while advancing U.S. interests and democratic norms and values. Despite our small interview pool, the experiences provided some key lessons from the past five years of implementation from which to build on.

Throughout our research, we were most often directed to the CCMD GENADs for success stories, highlighting the impact of GENADs. WPS principles are understood by the service members with whom we spoke, who linked the implementation of these principles to operational successes. Moreover, these successes beget further understanding of WPS and ideas for how to implement it in the future. For example, lessons learned from OAW and working with a large refugee population are being shared with INDOPACOM partner nations that either support peacekeeping operations or manage large numbers of refugees within their borders. Bangladeshi military officials reached out to INDOPACOM specifically asking about any experience with internally displaced people and refugees, as the result of command messaging. Interviewees noted that "OAW gave us the credibility with our military counterparts [in other countries]," which has provided INDOPACOM more opportunities to engage with and support capacity building of partners.[27] In 2022, the INDOPACOM GENADs developed training on how to integrate WPS principles into refugee operations, building on OAW lessons learned.[28]

In another positive takeaway, we found that despite many people generally equating WPS implementation with the work being done specifically by GENADs, our interviews also anecdotally highlighted that a gender-diverse and inclusive culture is building in DoD from the bottom up. The Civil Affairs human trafficking training course occurred not only because the junior officer had the idea but also because of the support of successive commanders, both men and women.[29] In SOUTHCOM, support for WPS education and training has come from two male command sergeant majors.[30] Multiple women with

43

Capt. Carolyn Currie conducts a WPS seminar with Guatemalan service members on October 28, 2022, aboard the hospital ship USNS Comfort.

experience in the special operations community noted how male allies used specific examples of how gender diversity improved operational success to convince skeptical operators of the need for increased inclusivity.[31] One of these interviewees recounted a conversation with former Special Operations Command commander GEN Richard D. Clarke, in which he acknowledged, "Everywhere I look, everyone looks like me and I know it isn't good. We don't have the right conversations as a result."[32] Most interviewees indicated that the support of leaders, commanders, and male allies is critical to the widespread understanding and success of WPS principles.

Despite the successes of operationalizing and implementing WPS principles across DoD, our interviews revealed a few potential areas for improvement to ensure their continued implementation. Of note, as DoD works to improve women's inclusion and equity within the department and across the services, challenging the status quo can provoke a backlash. In a 2016 RAND study, researchers found that "there is strong, deep-seated, and intensely felt opposition to opening [Special Operations Forces] specialties that have been closed to women" (Szayna et al., 2016). In early 2017, the Marines United scandal broke, with the public learning of a males-only, private Facebook group that maintained an archive of photographs of identifiable female service members in various stages of undress (Januta, 2017). As DoD continues to implement WPS principles, it should be aware of this potential for backlash and work to mitigate such a response.

Training

Although the 2017 WPS Act and the DoD WPS SFIP have provided a foundation and general framework for DoD and its implementation of WPS principles, our interviews anecdotally revealed the lack of a unified theory as to why approaches and perspectives that account for gender matter to DoD and the benefits of implementing WPS principles.[33] Training for the force, with specific examples of WPS in action across all levels of DoD activities, will reinforce the successes of the past five years and the grassroots efforts being seen.

Barriers

In many instances, women have been enablers of U.S. military operations versus directly participating in operations or combat. Therefore, these combat arms communities face challenges in diversifying the experiences and perspectives of those who are invited to sit at the table and listened to once present. Developing cadres of female team members and leaders in these fields will take time but should be encouraged in parallel with active efforts to include diverse perspectives in the meantime. For example, when a new commander arrives, that person brings along a staff that often has a similar background, such as flying the same aircraft type or being in a particular special operations training course. If women are not represented in those military communities, it is difficult for them to gain a seat at the table. And if they are included, they are often further marginalized as they lack the background shared by the rest of the staff.[34] Many of our interviewees noted the lack of senior officers who are women in the rooms where strategic decisions are made. In a discussion about CSTs and Female Engagement Teams, one interviewee commented, "We only brought in American women to engage with Afghan women to the extent where men are not allowed to. Women are not there to set the policy. When it comes to decisionmaking, policy, and strategy, women are not involved."[35]

Security Cooperation

Many of our partners are paying attention when the United States emphasizes the importance of considering gender perspectives and are working to improve their implementation of WPS principles. However, they also notice when we do not "walk the walk"—for example, during a training exercise in Eastern Europe, where a young foreign officer demanded to know why there were no American women present.[36] As strategic competition comes to the fore, our partners in the Indo-Pacific region and South America recognize the difference between our competitors' actions versus representative democratic values that respect human rights. As one GENAD noted, "It's strategic, but also humane,"[37] while another noted that gender diversity is a pathway to democracy, which in turn is a powerful influence against coercion and our competitors.[38] Increasing training on and inclusion of WPS principles is a powerful tool to build support and influence among our partners. By contrast, adherence to traditional gender norms in U.S. military operations and activities will likely undermine the success of American national security objectives broadly if partners and allies do not see the U.S. military implementing principles it encourages them to apply.

The Way Ahead

Throughout this report, we have highlighted some of the successes achieved in integrating WPS principles into DoD operations. However, we have also highlighted areas where our interviewees noted room for improvement within the department. In some cases, our vignettes illustrated the implementation of WPS principles in operational and tactical environments before the WPS Act was passed, indicating that DoD has been considering such an approach even before official changes in policy.

Since 2017, the operating environment for the U.S. military has changed. U.S. forces departed Afghanistan and have a limited deployed presence in Iraq and Syria. Strategic competition against China and Russia is now the national security priority, which provides opportunities to implement WPS principles across military operations to counter those countries' growing influence. INDOPACOM and SOUTHCOM's work with the PDC, for example, shows how applying gender perspectives to partner engagements and operations can improve relationships and increase our influence. OAW was a successful proof of concept of incorporating gender perspectives in the planning of the operation versus a piecemeal effort, providing clear connections between mission success and WPS principles. In the next five years, efforts to expand the work of GENADs should continue, along with building a culture within DoD that aligns with WPS principles, the WPS Act, and the SFIP. Progress toward achieving the lines of effort should be measured, along with identifying specific actions to fill any gaps between line-of-effort objectives and the current state of implementation. Moreover, following the protests over systemic racial injustice in 2020, discussions surrounding diversity, equity, and inclusion have highlighted the criticality of intersectionality—that is, considering more than one social categorization (e.g., gender, class, race, or religion) at a time—in WPS implementation (Yeung and Lim, 2021). As DoD's implementation of WPS continues, intersectionality should be at the forefront.

As academic and Swedish Army reservist Robert Egnell notes, "The issue of women in combat should not be approached through the lens of damage control, but rather with an emphasis on maximizing the effectiveness of military organizations in the contemporary strategic context" (Egnell, 2013). DoD's identification and prioritization of strategic competition puts the focus on operating spaces that build relationships and influence over the likelihood of interstate conflict. Considering gender perspectives when interacting with foreign partners and within the U.S. military will provide opportunities to highlight shared values at the expense of adversaries. Diversity of representation within the force will allow the United States to be more responsive, flexible, and innovative to achieve DoD's missions in defense of the nation.

Abbreviations

AFSOC	Air Force Special Operations Command
AU	African Union
CCMD	combatant command
CENTCOM	Central Command
CSO	combat systems officer
CST	cultural support teams
DHS	U.S. Department of Homeland Security
DoD	U.S. Department of Defense
DSCA	Defense Support of Civil Authorities
FTP	Female Tactical Platoon
GDF	Guyana Defence Force
GENAD	gender adviser
HKIA	Hamid Karzai International Airport
INDOPACOM	Indo-Pacific Command
ISR	intelligence, surveillance, and reconnaissance
JFC	Joint Force Command
NATO	North Atlantic Treaty Organization
NGO	nongovernmental organization
NORTHCOM	Northern Command
NSD-Hub	NATO Strategic Direction South Hub
OAIs	operations, activities, and investments
OAW	Operation Allies Welcome
OSD	Office of the Secretary of Defense
PDC	Pacific Disaster Center
RSM	Resolute Support Mission
SCO	Security Cooperation Office
SFIP	Strategic Framework and Implementation Plan
SIV	Special Immigration Visa
SOF	special operations forces
SOJTF-OIR	Special Operations Joint Task Force Operation-Inherent Resolve
SOUTHCOM	Southern Command
TIP	Trafficking in Persons
UNSCR	United Nations Security Council Resolution
WPS	Women, Peace and Security

References

Allen, Molly, Mir Ashfaquzzaman, Megan Bryan, Gabby Estlund, Mehrnaz Khanjani, Maria Kuiper, Kathryn Raver, Nichole Shaw, and Olivia Williams, *Women and Water in the Developing World: Linking Water Insecurity and Gender Disparities*, Center for Strategic and International Studies Journalism Bootcamp, September 30, 2020.

Angelo, Paul J., "Another Conflict is Brewing in the Caribbean," *Foreign Policy*, March 22, 2022.

Balon, Bojana, Anna Björsson, Tanja Geiss, Aiko Holvikivi, Anna Kadar, Iryna Lysychkina, and Callum Watson, *Teaching Gender in the Military: A Handbook*, Geneva Centre for Security Sector Governance, 2016.

Bohan, Janis, "Regarding Gender: Essentialism, Constructionism, and Feminist Psychology," *Psychology of Women Quarterly*, Vol. 17, 1993, pp. 5–21.

Chenoweth, Erica, and Zoe Marks, "Revenge of the Patriarchs: Why Autocrats Fear Women," *Foreign Affairs*, March/April 2022.

Connelly, Michael F., and Jean D. Clandinin, "Stories of Experience and Narrative Inquiry," *Educational Researcher*, Vol. 19, No. 5, 1990, pp. 2–14.

Datta, Monti, Angharad Smith, and Kevin Bales, "Slavery and War Are Tightly Connected—But We Had No Idea Just How Much Until We Crunched the Data," *The Conversation*, August 22, 2022.

Dewaal, Alex, "The African Union and the Libya Conflict of 2011," World Peace Foundation, December 19, 2012.

DHS—*See* U.S. Department of Homeland Security.

Eddy, Max, "Women Utterly Destroy Men in Social Engineering Competition," *PC Magazine*, November 8, 2013.

Egnell, Robert, "Women in Battle: Gender Perspectives and Fighting," *Parameters*, Vol. 43, No. 2, Summer 2013.

Egnell, Robert, "Gender Perspectives and Military Effectiveness: Implementing UNSCR 1325 and the National Action Plan on Women, Peace and Security," *PRISM*, Vol. 6, No. 1, March 1, 2016.

Fathi, Nazila, "In a Death Seen Around the World, a Symbol of Iranian Protests," *New York Times*, June 22, 2009.

Filkins, Dexter, "The Exiled Dissent Fuelling the Hijab Protests in Iran," *New Yorker*, September 24, 2022.

Garamone, Jim, "National Security Strategy Aims to Address New Challenges," *DOD News*, October 13, 2022.

Heinecken, Lindy, "Conceptualizing the Tensions Evoked by Gender Integration in the Military," *Armed Forces and Society*, Vol. 43, No. 2, 2017, pp. 202–220.

Hudson, Valerie M., Donna Lee Bowen, and Perpetua Lynne Nelson, *The First Political Order: How Sex Shapes Governance and National Security Worldwide*, Columbia University Press, 2020.

Januta, Andrea, "How the Marines United Investigation and Scandal Unfolded," *The War Horse*, July 11, 2017.

Joint Doctrine Note 1-19, Competition Continuum, June 3, 2019.

Karim, Sabrina, and Kyle Beardsley, *Equal Opportunity Peacekeeping: Women, Peace, and Security in Post-Conflict States*, Oxford University Press, 2017.

Katt, Megan, "Blurred Lines: Cultural Support Teams in Afghanistan," *Joint Force Quarterly*, Vol. 75, October 2014, pp. 106–113.

Krause, Jana, Werner Krause, and Piia Bränfors, "Women's Participation in Peace Negotiations and the Durability of Peace," *International Interactions*, Vol. 44, No. 4, August 2018, pp. 1–32.

McNierney, Brooke A., "Female Engagement Teams: An Evaluation of The Female Engagement Team Program in Afghanistan," in *Constructive Pathways: Stimulating and Safeguarding Components of WPS*, April 2015.

North Atlantic Treaty Organization, "NATO and Libya (Archived)," webpage, November 9, 2015. As of September 28, 2022:
https://www.nato.int/cps/en/natohq/topics_71652.htm

O'Reilly, Marie, "Inclusive Security and Peaceful Societies: Exploring the Evidence," *PRISM*, Vol. 6, No. 1, March 1, 2016.

Peterson, Scott, "'This Girl Has United Us All': Women's Rage Mobilizes Iranians," *Christian Science Monitor*, September 23, 2022.

Prescott, Jody M., "Climate Change, Gender, and Rethinking Military Operations," *Vermont Journal of Environmental Law*, Vol. 15, No. 4, 2014, pp. 766–802.

Public Law 115-68, Women, Peace, and Security Act of 2017, Section 4, Statement of Policy, October 6, 2017.

Ripley, Amanda, "The Untold Story of the Afghan Women Who Hunted the Taliban," *Politico*, April 8, 2022.

Slapakova, Linda, Ben Caves, Marek N. Posard, Julia Muravska, Diana Dascalu, Diana Y. Myers, Raymond Kuo, and Kristin Thue, *Leveraging Diversity For Military Effectiveness: Diversity, Inclusion and Belonging in the UK and US Armed Forces*, RAND Corporation, RR-A1026-1, 2022. As of September 28, 2022:
https://www.rand.org/pubs/research_reports/RRA1026-1.html

Steinmetz, Kevin F., Alexandra Pimentel, and W. Richard Goe, "Performing Social Engineering: A Qualitative Study of Information Security Deceptions," *Computers in Human Behavior*, Vol. 124, No. 3, June 2021.

Szayna, Thomas S., Eric V. Larson, Angela O'Mahony, Sean Robson, Agnes Gereben Schaefer, Miriam Matthews, J. Michael Polich, Lynsay Ayer, Derek Eaton, William Marcellino, Lisa Kraus, Marek N. Posard, James Syme, Zev Winkelman, Cameron Wright, Megan Zander Cotugno, and William Welser IV, *Considerations for Integrating Women into Closed Occupations in U.S. Special Operations Forces*, RAND Corporation, RR-1058-USSOCOM, 2016. As of February 1, 2023:
https://www.rand.org/pubs/research_reports/RR1058.html

Tracy, Jared M., "The U.S. Army Cultural Support Team Program: Historical Timeline," *Veritas*, Vol. 12, No. 2, 2016.

United Nations, "International Day of the Abolition of Slavery, 2 December," webpage, undated. As of September 27, 2022:
https://www.un.org/en/observances/slavery-abolition-day

United Nations High Commissioner for Refugees, "Growing Concerns for Syrian Civilians Amid Intense Fighting in Al Raqqa and Deir ez-Zor," webpage, October 13, 2017. As of September 28, 2022:
https://www.unhcr.org/en-us/news/briefing/2017/10/59e07b5d4/growing-concerns-syrian-civilians-amid-intense-fighting-al-raqqa-deir-ez.html

United Nations Security Council Resolution 1325, "On Women and Peace and Security," October 31, 2000.

United States Institute of Peace, "Advancing Women, Peace and Security: U.S. Civil Society Working Group on Women, Peace & Security (U.S. CSWG)," webpage, undated. As of February 15, 2023:
https://www.usip.org/programs/advancing-women-peace-and-security#:~:text=Women%2C%20Peace%20and%20Security%20(WPS,peace%20processes%2C%20peacebuilding%20and%20security

University of Nottingham, "Rights Lab," webpage, undated. As of September 28, 2022:
https://www.nottingham.ac.uk/research/beacons-of-excellence/rights-lab/index.aspx

U.S. Central Command, "Senior Official Outlines U.S. missions in Afghanistan," webpage, May 6, 2016. As of September 28, 2022:
https://www.centcom.mil/MEDIA/NEWS-ARTICLES/News-Article-View/Article/885352/senior-official-outlines-us-missions-in-afghanistan/

U.S. Department of Defense, *Women, Peace, and Security Strategic Implementation Framework and Implementation Plan*, June 2020.

U.S. Department of Homeland Security, "Operation Allies Welcome," webpage, undated. As of September 29, 2022:
https://www.dhs.gov/allieswelcome

U.S. Department of State, "2021 Trafficking in Persons Report: Venezuela," website, undated-a. As of October 11, 2022:
https://www.state.gov/reports/2021-trafficking-in-persons-report/venezuela/

U.S. Department of State, "*The Department of State's Plan to Implement the U.S. Strategy on Women, Peace, and Security*," webpage, undated-b. As of February 17, 2023:
https://www.state.gov/the-department-of-states-plan-to-implement-the-u-s-strategy-on-women-peace-and-security/

U.S. Department of State, "Women, Peace and Security," webpage, undated-c. As of April 6, 2023:
https://www.state.gov/women-peace-and-security/

U.S. Senate, letter addressed to U.S. Secretary of State Antony Blinken and U.S. Secretary of Homeland Security Alejandro Mayorkas, August 16, 2021.

U.S. Southern Command, "Tradewinds 2021," webpage, undated. As of September 29, 2022:
https://www.southcom.mil/Media/Special-Coverage/Tradewinds-2021/

White House, *United States Government Women, Peace, and Security*, June 2019.

White House, *United States Government Women, Peace, and Security (WPS) Congressional Report*, June 2021.

White House, *United States Government Women, Peace, and Security (WPS) Congressional Report*, July 2022a.

White House, *National Security Strategy*, October 2022b.

Women's International League for Peace and Freedom, "United States of America," webpage, undated. As of February 15, 2023:
http://1325naps.peacewomen.org/index.php/united-states-of-america/

Yeung, Douglas, and Nelson Lim, eds., *Perspectives on Diversity, Equity, and Inclusion in the Department of the Air Force,* RAND Corporation, PE-A909-1, November 2021. As of February 1, 2023:
https://www.rand.org/pubs/perspectives/PEA909-1.html

About This Research Report

In light of the five-year anniversary of the Women, Peace, and Security Act of 2017, the RAND Corporation sought to understand strategic, operational, and tactical applications of Women, Peace, and Security (WPS) principles in the U.S. Department of Defense (DoD) operations and activities. A series of vignettes highlights specific efforts to implement DoD's WPS Strategic Framework and Implementation Plan within the military services and during operations with allies and partners. Although the most successful efforts to implement WPS principles are directly tied to specific policies and initiatives, a growing gender-diverse and inclusive culture within DoD supports grassroots efforts to apply gender perspectives to DoD activities and operations. Despite the successes of operationalizing and implementing WPS across DoD, room for improvement exists to ensure the continued implementation of WPS principles to support U.S. military activities and operations that require diverse perspectives and flexibility to confront adversaries in a competitive environment.

RAND National Security Research Division

This research was sponsored by the Office of the Secretary of Defense for Policy and conducted within the International Security and Defense Policy Center of the RAND National Security Research Division (NSRD), which operates the National Defense Research Institute (NDRI), a federally funded research and development center sponsored by the Office of the Secretary of Defense, the Joint Staff, the Unified Combatant Commands, the Navy, the Marine Corps, the defense agencies, and the defense intelligence enterprise.

The research reported here was completed in January 2023 and underwent security review with the sponsor and the Defense Office of Prepublication and Security Review before public release.

For more information on the RAND International Security and Defense Policy Center, see www.rand.org/nsrd/isdp or contact the director (contact information is provided on the webpage).

Acknowledgments

We are grateful to the support from our sponsor, the Office for the Secretary Defense for Policy; the Office for Strategy, Plans and Capabilities; and the Office for Global Partnerships, especially Siena Cicarelli, Erin Cooper, and Cori Fleser. We would be remiss if we did not acknowledge our former RAND Corporation colleagues, Jeannette Haynie and Agnes Schaefer, for developing this idea and setting us on the correct path. We also thank our interviewees for their candor in discussing the successes and challenges faced in their professional experiences. Kyleanne Hunter of RAND and Hilary Matfess of the University of Denver provided insightful and helpful comments during their thorough reviews of this report. All errors remain the responsibility of the authors. Special thanks to Katherine Wu for her extraordinary design.

Notes

[1] For updated versions of the report, see U.S. Department of State, undated-c.

[2] The RAND National Security Research Division's standardized human subjects research screening methods, developed in collaboration with RAND's Institutional Review Board, deemed this to not constitute "human subjects" research. Nonetheless, all interviews are attributed anonymously throughout this report in compliance with the U.S. Federal Policy for the Protection of Human Subjects (also known as the Common Rule). Although interviewees were asked to respond based on their professional experiences, they were, in all cases, speaking for themselves rather than for their organizations in an official capacity.

[3] For the purpose of this research, *vignettes* are defined as a brief account or story of a personal experience that weave together a series of events and are built from interviews with one to two participants. The use of narrative inquiry in qualitative research has been demonstrated to reveal detail about situations or lived experiences (see Connelly and Clandinin, 1990, pp. 2–14.)

[4] Of note, through snowball sampling, we were often directed toward gender advisers in the services or at the GCCs. Anecdotal comments from our interviews indicate a potential trend of informally equating WPS with gender advisers throughout DoD. This could potentially indicate that WPS has not fully been operationalized in DoD. Further research is necessary to understand this relationship and the impact on implementing WPS principles.

[5] *Gender essentialism* refers to the belief there is an underlying and immutable essence to gender that defines a person and may not be affected by sociopolitical factors (Bohan, 1993).

[6] Although lacking a definition in international law, *modern slavery* is a broad term that includes such practices as forced labor, debt bondage, forced marriage, and human trafficking (see United Nations, undated).

[7] This vignette is based on an interview with a defense official, July 21, 2022. All direct quotes in this vignette are from this interview unless noted otherwise. The timeline for U.S. withdrawal was further extended, with the last remaining forces in Afghanistan departing by September 1, 2021.

[8] U.S. Central Command, "Senior Official Outlines U.S. Missions in Afghanistan," webpage, May 6, 2016.

[9] This vignette is based on an interview with three different defense officials on April 25, 2022, May 16, 2021, and June 2, 2022. Direct quotes in this vignette are attributed to these specific interviews.

[10] Interview with defense official, June 2, 2022.

[11] Interview with defense official, May 16, 2021.

[12] This vignette is based on an interview with a defense official, May 17, 2022. All direct quotes in this vignette are from this interview unless noted otherwise.

[13] Interview with a defense official on May 17, 2022.

[14] This vignette is based on an interview with a defense official on May 18, 2022, and a follow-up interview on July 27, 2022. Additional information was provided during an interview with analysts from an applied research center on June 7, 2022. Direct quotes in this vignette are attributed to these specific interviews.

[15] Interview with a defense official on May 18, 2022.

[16] Trafficking in persons falls within DoD's purview because it is interlinked with cross-border security and the movement of illegal goods.

[17] Interview with a defense official on May 18, 2022.

[18] Interview with a defense official on May 18, 2022.

19 This vignette is based on an interview with a defense official, April 29, 2022. All direct quotes in this vignette are from this interview unless noted otherwise.

20 Interview with a defense official on July 21, 2022.

21 This anecdote is based on an interview with a former defense official, August 9, 2022. All direct quotes in this anecdote are from this interview unless noted otherwise.

22 This anecdote is based on an interview with a former defense official, May 17, 2022. All direct quotes in this anecdote are from this interview unless noted otherwise.

23 This anecdote is based on an interview with a defense official, April 27, 2022. All direct quotes in this anecdote are from this interview unless noted otherwise.

24 The courses are also reviewed and refined by subject-matter experts from DoD's Countering Trafficking in Persons Program Management Office, Department of State, and the Defense Security Cooperation University's Institute for Security Governance.

25 This anecdote is based on an interview with a former defense official, June 7, 2022. All direct quotes in this anecdote are from this interview unless noted otherwise.

26 The NSD-Hub is a NATO framework that focuses on ensuring regional stability in Africa and the Middle East through better understanding of threats and challenges emanating from those regions.

27 Interview with a defense official, May 18, 2022, and July 27, 2022.

28 Interview with a defense official, May 18, 2022, and July 27, 2022.

29 Interview with a defense official, April 27, 2022.

30 Interview with a defense official, May 16, 2022.

31 Interview with a former defense official, April 22, 2022.

32 Interview with a defense official, May 24, 2022.

33 Interview with defense officials, May 4, 2022; Interview with a former defense official, April 22, 2022.

34 Interview with a former defense official, April 22, 2022; Interview with a defense official, May 16, 2022.

35 Interview with a former defense official, April 22, 2022.

36 Interview with defense officials, May 4, 2022.

37 Interview with a defense official, May 16, 2022.

38 Interview with a defense official, May 18, 2022, and July 27, 2022.